Fulfilling Your Hearts Desires

The Choice is Yours

By: Books of the Heart
E.L. Hutton

Gotham Books

30 N Gould St.
Ste. 20820, Sheridan, WY 82801
https://gothambooksinc.com/

Phone: 1 (307) 464-7800

© 2023 *E.L. Hutton*. All rights reserved.

No part of this book may be reproduced, stored in a retrieval system, or transmitted by any means without the written permission of the author.

Published by Gotham Books (August 24, 2023)

ISBN: 979-8-88775-471-0 (P)
ISBN: 979-8-88775-472-7 (E)

Because of the dynamic nature of the Internet, any web addresses or links contained in this book may have changed since publication and may no longer be valid.

The views expressed in this work are solely those of the author and do not necessarily reflect the views of the publisher, and the publisher hereby disclaims any responsibility for them.

TABLE OF CONTENTS

CHAPTER	TITLE	PAGE#
01	Life Begins	07
02	Empowered by Thoughts	18
02.1	My Story	24
03	Joys of Youth	28
04	What Are You Thinking?	35
05	Stopping in Your Tracks	38
06	The Voice	42
07	Where is God?	46
08	The Hospital	54
09	When You Listen!	58
10	Believing is a Practice	61
11	Pay Attention to What You're Saying	67
12	Your Own Computer	70
13	Affirming Happiness	74
14	The Hearts Desire	82
15	Finding Your Way	85
16	The Apple Orchard	89
17	Three Years Later	95
18	Doing What You Love	98

PREFACE

The title of the book is to get your attention. I want you to realize that you are in control of your future. We have the gift to create and to have what we want in life. It all really begins in the way we think. Where do these thoughts come from? What do they create in our own life?

Does doubt, and a feeling of being unworthy take you to negative thinking? Such as hearing ourself saying, "I have no friends. People just do not like me"?

Our self-talk affects the way we live our life and directs us on how to proceed.

It is the intention of this book to give you a pathway that will work. This book will help you to master your life and to deal with the experiences and beliefs that do not serve you well.

It is my hope that you will all become masters of your life and heart's desires. This is my gift to you and your gift to your life.

If you have not read the previous book to this one, I encourage you to get a copy of it:

"AND SO IT IS,_Begin to Change Your Life Right Now!" It was written under the Pen name of Lynne Wilson

This book teaches you how to change your life and be able to understand affirmations and how they can truly work. When you learn to use them regularly you will begin to see that you can have what you want in life. You must always remember not to follow up your affirmation with a negative thoughts or words.

If you are stubborn as I am and was, you will find yourself in a battle with negative thoughts. Just think and follow what you are taught in this book, and you will find things go smoother.

I have had many tell me that they carry the book, *"And So It Is"* with them, and it helps them have more peace.

CHAPTER
I

Life
BEGINS

When we are babies, we learn instinctively how to get our mother's attention. It seems that they arrived with this ability to make sounds, like crying, and giggling to let us know they want our attention.

I have found that whenever a baby giggles or smiles at me they have my attention. It automatically makes me smile and experience joy. When our baby cries and we don't know why, we quickly jump into action to see what is going on with our child.

When they cry, it is a signal that they need our attention, whether it needs to be held, or diapered or fed. We are at their beck and call as they graduate from babyhood to becoming small children. The life of a child is a big responsibility for a mother, and we really do need to be disciplined in what we do.

This also applies to our everyday thinking. It seems so easy to go negative and then physically we feel the recourse from it. The negative gets us thinking about all the things that we don't like or want in our life.

The reward from thinking outside of the feeling box is great! As we watch our children grow up, we must keep our minds on the fact that they are learning. Are these trying times? Yes! Especially, as they are growing and are in the process of finding out how to get their way.

The gift of being a mother comes with all kinds of rewards and challenges, as all of you who are mothers know this. As a mom our time is usually occupied with our children. Just keep in mind that we will be rewarded as our children grow up.

For myself it was tough when they wanted to go and hang out with the other kids and most times problems would arise. Only, because we have had to let go of 24-hour surveillance.

The bottom line is that raising children teaches us repetition, discipline in our day, and the fortitude not to give up. At the end of all of this, you may have great children who grow up and give you grandchildren.

You don't have to take over, but you can enjoy loving moments and smiles with your grandchildren. Smile…

Children are a gift to parents who have chosen to bring life into this world. It is a blessed event that says you have been chosen to give life, love, and happiness to a gift from God that has been given to you as a blessing. This gift has been given to you for a purpose.

I would like to insert here that parents came as a man and women figure because each had their own gifts and things to teach their children who would be born as male or female. Each having certain things that they were to teach their children.

Now you might say that "well, things are different now". No, the truth still stands and if stood by and followed brings happiness.

The thoughts of change in what God intended, is only the doings of Satan taking over the world and destroying all the beauty and the gifts of life that God had in mind for mankind when the earth was first created.

Men and women were created in different roles so that there would be a balance and happiness in the life that we were to have. Male and Female whether it be people or animals all were created to populate the earth.

The Earth was created with guidelines and rules that really make everything work. When it comes to being a man and a woman figure, in your child's life. this is so that the female and male can teach each of their children the way to have a good and happy life. The male comes with certain gifts to teach the children how to have a good life and the woman has great responsibility in teaching how to love, be kind a good person. All of this is a responsibility that men have as well, only on a different level.

Some will say it's old history and things are different. The truth is that the beginning of this earth was for man and women to have a good life and to bring children in to become loving, kind, and good people for mankind and the earth.

In the days of my childhood God created a man and a woman for creating people in the world and man had his role as a provider and women had their role as a caretaker and nurturer.

Being a parent is a big job, however we must do our best to be there and to love and care for these little people that God felt we could take care of and love. Every person has a reason for being on earth and we must honor that we were chosen to come to earth.

I know many of you right now are saying things like, "you didn't come from the life I had; I had no choice." These are all the negative types of thinking that come to our mind to make us feel we are alone and there is no one there to help you. There is a shift that we will talk about as we go forward in this book that will help you understand.

When God allowed the small seed in you to become a child, it wasn't to punish anyone it was to give you love and something you could be proud of. When our ego jumps in the way, it will run rampant, if we agree to go with it. You are a gift to this world on many levels you may not even recognize or feel.

The fact that we can carry a small seed within our body and can feel it moving inside of us and communicating with us is a very powerful example of how much our higher consciousness creates in our life.

It is interesting that our babies' bond with us before they are born. I have had pregnant mothers tell me, "He's sleeping now".

At times he will be moving around in the mother's stomach, and she will automatically rub her stomach soothing the baby and she automatically will talk to the baby and the baby seems to respond.

This connection is a miracle when we are communicating with our child before it ever enters this world. That is how we know that God has a hand in this creation. It is all about Love and Kindness.

Listening to the inner voice of God brings a higher consciousness to you that will assist and protect you. You just need to learn how to listen and key in to living on your highest and best level.

As parents we must take our eyes off ourselves and teach love by bonding and giving a big part of ourselves to treasure and enhance the life of our child.

A child will give you what it learns from you. If you are anxious the baby whines and cries, if you are laughing the baby smiles. You have been given a wonderful gift of love you just have to treasure it. Realize it is watching and depending on you and learning how to be by your actions.

As small children, they watch and repeat what we say and do. If you use a swear word a lot, soon you will find that your child is now saying that word. You get angry and he/she gets upset because you discipline them. They idolize you and think if you do it, they should too.

Enough of this I just want you to understand about life and how we have more control over it than we think.

I know some are saying, "you probably didn't come from a negative life". This is exactly what our mind does to control us in negative ways.

CHAPTER II

Empowered
BY THOUGHTS

All people on earth must learn how to be happy. This is where what we are taught as a child is so important.

The big challenge is to not look backward with sadness and regret but to look forward to what is the good you can do and give in this world.

Living a life with discipline helps everyone to reach their goals and find happiness. Discipline must teach structure and does not come into one's life to teach pain or fear.

Would a child be upset when they must sit in a corner? Possibly, they will learn that being unruly results in not getting their way.

We must teach our children that there is a choice. We can pay the price of misbehaving, or we can reap the reward of choosing to do what is a right and good decision. It is a huge responsibility being a parent.

However, if you look at life in all ways, it is totally about learning how to do new things and have new experiences, whether it is having patience or being determined to accomplish something. It can even be planning a goal for the future. I have learned over the years that without structure we fall and must pick ourselves up quite a bit. We seem to create memories that we wish we did not have, and usually it comes from laziness and being unsure of what we have chosen to do.

LIFE A CHALLENGE
& A BLESSING

Beauty is in the Eye of the Beholder.

As a baby we come into the world usually crying, as we begin to take in air and breathe, and are probably wondering what is going on! Mommy takes us in her arms, and we feel the warmth of the blanket and our mothers' arms supporting us. Suddenly, we feel better and become calm.

A child forms its life from what it learns from the parents when they are very young. There is no one that will love us more than our children. We must teach them what will bring smiles and happiness into their life.

MY / STORY

As a child, I never for one moment thought that if I wanted to climb the biggest tree or go sleep in the doghouse with dog. that it would have a negative outcome.

Perhaps it was because I never heard negative reasons or things that would tell me that I could not do whatever it was that I wanted.

I lived in the desert and played with spiders and insects and never got a sting or bite. Lucky, for me. I wonder sometimes if it was just that I was never told anything negative about it. You see, as a child we usually have no fear.

I remember my father showing me the spiders, black widows, scorpions, not a spider, tarantulas that could jump on you very easily and make you very ill, or a least with a bad sting.,. I learned what they looked like and stayed clear of them because I had listened to what my father told me and stayed away from them.

My sister, brother and I knew that if my dad said so, it was true, and I never thought to go against what he said. It probably saved my life without me knowing it.

In our home from the time, we were born we knew that what Mom and Dad said was so. Arguing, fighting, and talking back never came into our life. I think we were very lucky, as our parents never argued or fought.

We had rules set for us, that we knew if we broke them that we would be in trouble. Interestingly, we never challenged or broke the rules our parents set for us. It never crossed our minds.

Now remember, when I was young the world was a much gentler place, and most people grew up knowing about rules and guidelines that made a better life for all.

However, as a child, I did grow up climbing huge trees and doing a lot of things that I could have had a bad experience from and injured.

I remember a time that my dad was working in the yard next to a shed that we had, and I climbed up a ladder and got on the roof. I told him, "I'm going to jump!"

He said, "It's going to hurt your feet". I said, "I'm jumping!". I jumped and it hurt my feet and I cried and told him I was telling Mom!

He just did not say a word and I didn't tell Mom. My father knew the shed was not big enough for me to really get hurt but it was a good lesson for me. I never jumped off the roof of anything after that.

However, I believe that the fact that I had no negative thinking going on it protected me. (My thoughts only, as I examine my life).

CHAPTER
III

Joys of YOUTH

When I was young, I could do anything I wanted: I played baseball in school, field hockey, all sports and never doubted that I could do it, so I tried just about everything. However, I did make decisions by what I liked most.

When I was in 7th grade, I played on a girls' baseball team. I really liked it, and I naturally did not think about whether I knew how to play or not. I just played and watched what others did and did the same thing.

When we tried out and I could catch, throw to homebase from outfield and catch the ball. I was on the team!

I did a lot of things. I think it was just because I never doubted myself or what I was doing. I never really thought about failing.

There was a time that I remember messing up as short stop and missing a catch that was a big deal for my team when it came to winning or losing this certain game.

No one really said anything negative to me, but my inner mind immediately convinced me that I was not a good ball player and probably shouldn't be playing.

The final game of the season came up the following week and my mom asked me if I was going to the game?   I immediately replied, "No, I'm not a very good player and if I don't play our team will win."

My mom didn't push me to go or say anything. We did not go to the game. My team won and then I knew that I was right. No one tried to convince me otherwise.   I never played ball again.

This is an example of how powerful our thoughts are and how quickly negative self-talk will jump in and convince us what is not true. The truth is that we are capable of anything we believe to be true. We must watch our thoughts. Our minds create self-judgment and make us believe that we are not good enough or that something is impossible. We might find ourselves saying "Other people get the breaks, not me".

My mother went through the Depression of World War 2:

She was a young girl who came from living a wealthy life, to eating potatoes boiled every day and remembered the bread lines. She used to say "Everyone else gets the good things and we are always at the end of the breadline. She carried this with her throughout life. In her adult life with my father she had a very good life lacking nothing during her marriage to my father, if she wanted it, she got it. Yet because of the embedded thinking of lack. It didn't matter how good her life was she only remember the past.

Mind you this woman was a star and on stage in New York when she was a child and had already accomplished many great things that she did not see, as this one phrase kept her blind from knowing that it was all waiting for her, but her focus on the negative phrase kept standing in the way of her belief system.

This is a bit of proof for you of how what we say keeps happening until we change our thoughts and focus on seeing what we want as happening or a possibility that it is on its way.

Never give up, when we say something negative, perhaps we might correct it by saying, "Another time, it will come to me". I would recommend that you quickly close your eyes and see yourself having what you want.

That statement alone will make a shift in your emotions and the way your body feels.

If ideas or pictures come into your mind about what you would do if you had the success you wanted. Let that thought be okay, don't end it with a comment or thought such as:

"No, others get to, but not me."

NEVER think or say that, as when you do you may begin to own the feeling.

We all have throughout life negative thoughts that we must become aware of. We must learn to quickly cancel these thoughts with something better. E*xample:* Replace it with *"My time will come at the perfect time"* or *"The next time I step up all will be perfect and grand for me."* Stand by it and believe it.

The important thing is to not follow the positive thought with any doubt:

Like perhaps ending it with *'I Hope"* or maybe you follow it with, *"Maybe it will be my time."*

CHAPTER
IV

What are YOU THINKING?

Our thinking and reactions to the thoughts going through our mind are something we just automatically respond to. Here's an example:

You are driving to work, the traffic is heavy, and you are running late. We find that we are talking to ourselves saying:

"Great! Get out of my way you jerk"! You are going to make me have to deal with "Brun Hilda", the receptionist at the office, looking at her watch and saying, "10 minutes late again!"

Instantly, you now get a vision of her looking down and making a note of it in her login book. You have now just set your day to start negatively.

This kind of thinking instantly seems to come into our mind and set our day for us. Learn to say *"erase, erase. All is well in my life!" Smile and agree.*

Catch yourself when you are talking to yourself. Especially when you are in doubt or anger. Realize that this thought or statement is not true, and simply declare. *"Erase, cancel. All things will work out better than I think."*

Remember to start every day with a positive thought such as **"*Today, everything goes right and perfect. And So, It Is.***

I always add in "**Thank you, thank you, all is well**".

After a time of a hard pattern of negative self-talk that seemed to take over parts of my life and brought me down and feeling hopeless. I started my day making this simple statement each morning and it instantly created a good day!

I will never forget to do this.

CHAPTER
V

Stopping in YOUR TRACKS!

Have you had one of those mornings when you just didn't want to go to work? Your mind begins to give you a lot of reasons why you should stay home, and you really would rather do anything but go to work.

I remember a time that I woke up one morning feeling lazy and just did not want to go to work. I found myself, looking in the mirror and saying,

"I don't feel good, I know I'm going to have a bad headache". There was a quiet voice within me saying "you have a project you need to finish today; you have to go".

Right away I turned to get dressed and had to sit on the bed because "My head started aching with my projected headache!" I said, "see I knew I was getting sick."

I promptly went and called in sick. The strange thing was once I made the call, I started to feel good! I pranced around and took the day off.

Little did I know that this important document job that needed finishing would be the result of possibly getting a raise.

When I went back the next day apologizing for not being there to finish the job I was working on and let them instantly know I would get it all done today.

My boss informed me that the person who completed my work did a great job and that she would be getting a bonus in her pay for being able to squeeze my job into her workload as well!

I said "a bonus? I didn't know that there was a bonus"?

He turned and informed me that it was a very important job, and a surprise for work well done. I didn't get the bonus and beat myself up for messing everything up, I sure could have used it.

The moral of the story is to listen to the quiet voice within and follow it. This is an example of how what we say creates what we experience.

CHAPTER
VI

The
VOICE

I know that many days I will look in the mirror and say, "Who in the World is that?" As I don't see a beautiful woman, I see the woman that has a brown spot on her face and gray hair growing in, and this image to me now looks quite old! From that moment on, more and more thoughts about aging begin to haunt me and reaffirm what I said about myself to the mirror. *Am I depressed?* Yes.

I will go shopping and find the greatest youth solutions that I can. It is good perhaps, if it is done in thought of making healthier skin for the woman in the mirror I criticized.

The correct thing to do is always take good care of ourselves We want to be dedicated to seeing the best of ourselves as well as others. From that moment on we will attract the kind of people and things we want into our life.

Our judgmental mind is not our friend when it is putting out the negative. What we said to ourselves in the mirror could have been "you may be older but you sure are a beauty"! Try doing this and you will see that a smile will automatically come to you. I will bet you just smiled!

Bottom line is stay positive and bring goodness into your life. Always speaking positively to others is especially important on both sides.

If you wake up tired and out of energy because you have been tossing and turning all night you will hear your mind giving you messages like, "you work hard most of the time, you deserve an extra day off" or you will hear that voice that says, "you don't need to go to work no one will miss you".

Now you start beating yourself up with "that's right probably no one will miss me."

Now you begin to feel like you are not worthy and good enough for people to care for. What a bummer… and you just laid it all on yourself and now you feel bad.

The truth is our Mind will feed us whatever we direct it to. If you get mad and throw something across the room and it smashes into pieces, you then may be saying "yep, that's right, one of my favorite things now is gone."

You never really intended to throw that thing and break something else, but it happened just to fulfill your negative thought.

CHAPTER VII

Where is GOD?

God is the great rescuer and source that has been with us since the Beginning of Time. He will never let us down. Mind you no matter what your religious or birth beliefs are, we all have a higher source that has power. For me it is God, for others it may be Buddha, or a label for the source of power and goodness from a belief in different countries of their God that they worship.

However, we do need to learn to listen to the little nudge or quiet voice that says, "don't do that." I'm not sure all religions note this, but it is something that is there no matter who you are that speaks softly to you in your mind.

I am going to share with you a perfect example of Listening to God:

I was in my 30's and was driving to have an interview with a Motel for a position working with them at the Desk when customers arrived to check in for their rooms. I was beginning to park out front of the hotel, I kept hearing this voice saying, *"don't take this job." "You don't need to do this."*

Now I knew that it was God telling me not to take the job. As I often did, *"I said it will be okay"* and ignored him. I must say this was the first time I heard his voice very loud protesting. I went in for the interview and got the job and had to sign an acceptance paper and this voice said, *"Don't Do This!"* I ignored it and went to work there. I liked the job.

About a month later I was working on a night shift and young man about 16yrs old came into the hotel and asked if I could give him change for a phone call he wanted to make.

I informed him that we didn't have much change, but since it was only a $5 dollar bill, it would be okay". I was looking down into the drawer to make change for the $5 bill he gave me, and I heard this quiet voice, strong and clear say to me while I was looking into the drawer,

"He has a gun do nothing."

I looked up and the boy had the gun in my face. I was not scared, and the voice said, "do what he says", I did. He came behind the counter and I stood in a doorway just away from the counter while he robbed us. I found myself feeling very sad for this young man who felt he had to do this. The kid kept saying <u>"shut up and stop talking."</u>

I remember saying *"I'm not talking."* At that moment I saw that I could rush him and push him to a closet and the voice loudly said *"No, Do Nothing."*

Without really reacting or noticing a White cloud wrapped around me and took me up out of the room and I was in a place that seemed like all clouds, and I was walking next to what I called or related to as God. He had an exceptionally soft but vivid voice that said come I want to show you something.

We walked over to a place that seemed high in the sky, yet it was like standing on the edge of a mountain. The voice said, "Look," as he waved his arm across the mass of clouds in front of us and they parted and opened into a clear valley below. At least, that is how I saw it.

I was amazed to see thousands, and thousands of people young and old weeping. He said to me:

"This is why I weep, for they are not listening and do not know the truth."

He turned me back toward the beam of light that we came on when we arrived at this place. He said:

"You can come here anytime. You do not need to do it this way."

I was returned to the room that I was standing in at the hotel where the guy in the room was standing with a gun pointed at my head. As the boy pulled the trigger and I watched him. I felt a hand on the back of my head gently tipping my head forward just as he pulled the trigger.

The boy was shocked when I did not fall to the floor, cry, or make any noise. He was horrified and ran out the front door.

I never fell to the floor or really realized that he did shoot me. I heard the sound, but it did not sink in, I was walking about talking and feeling no pain. I thought he missed and hit the cabinet behind me. I was walking around and went down to my manger's door, and she was not there.

When I came back to the area where he shot the gun, this voice said, "Stop walking around and call the police." I followed directions.

I called the police and told them our hotel name and that we had been robbed.

I did not know that I had been shot, until I happened to look down at my clothes and saw that I was covered with blood. I was not hysterical, I just remember looking and seeing my clothes covered in blood and saying, "oh no, this was one of my favorites."

It was then that I said to the officer; "Oh, I guess I've been shot in the head", she started screaming and I hung up the phone. It was only a few minutes, 2 to 5 min, before the police arrived. The Police department was about a block away. I never fell off my feet, cried or was scared.

I just remembered that, as I was watching the boy's finger on the trigger that it felt like a hand was on the back of my head and pushed my head forward a bit. I think that was what saved my life.

CHAPTER
VIII

The
HOSPITAL

While all of this was going on I was never afraid. I was taken by ambulance to the hospital. The doctor who checked me out stepped out of the room to get a nurse to wash my hair. All I heard was that my hair needed washing. A police officer was with me at the hospital. He never said anything to me, and I just got up and washed my own hair. When the doctor came in to sew me up. He asked me why I did that.

I simply said I thought I was supposed to do that. He shook his head and then began to look at my head so he could sew up the bullet wounds.

After a moment, He walked in front of me in shock. He was pale white, pointed to me and said, **"You are a miracle!"**

He said that when he started to get ready to sew up my wound, that he watched the skin come back together on my head just as if nothing had happened and that there was nothing for him to do. He shook his head and walked out of the room.

On that same night after shooting me, this Kid went on a spree and shot a storeowner in the chest and a woman walking down the street in the face.

He was arrested and was sentenced to 30 years to Life in Prison.

I tell you this story, as it is a way for me to show you that if I had listened when God had told me not to take the job, I never would have had this problem. (You may just think of it as the quiet inner voice). that said not to take the job. This Inner voice has always been there for me and protected me and saved me more than once.

I thank God, that in my life. I was very lucky that my belief was in God. I knew he would protect me, and I had him on my side. I naturally believed in him from the time I was a child and never really knew anything different. It seemed natural to me.

This is a demonstration how God works in our life. He has saved mine more than once.

CHAPTER IX

When You LISTEN!

If you listen to the quiet voice that is guarding you, you will recognize that he never leaves you, you will become very aware that he is always with you.

Many times, we don't listen to the soft voice that is very different than the loud shouting, unloving voice of Ego or you may call it Satan.

God has gone on walks with me and been with me always. Once you learn to listen and walk with him you will never be alone. It is only the mortals' world that pulls us off course.

All these rights are yours too if you believe. Talk to him and listen. You will know he is with you. He has done this with me *all of my life*.

When you talk with God and ask of him, he always listens and will deliver to you what is best for you to know or do. If you do not hear or sense a direct answer that is because he is waiting on you to listen or sense what he is saying.

I find that most times in the middle of night or the next day after I wake up, I will have a sign or know by what is happening that he is there.

Just give thanks for what you ask and then let go and you will see when you are not expecting it an answer or knowing has come to you.

He never leaves anyone unless they slam the door and block him out. You may not notice him, but he is watching and remembering the help you need. You must be willing to accept his gifts, or you will not realize it. Patience, patience, at the right time you will know that he is there. We cannot live on both sides of the street, we must choose.

CHAPTER X

Believing is A PRACTICE!

I learned that my belief in God all, of my life, from childhood up saved my life and wellbeing.

If you don't turn away from God, he will never turn away from you. This is a story to help you to understand that quiet voice. He is just waiting for you to believe in him and invite him into your life. I am not trying to convince you to ask God into your life, because I'm a believer. I just know that he stands by us always waiting to be invited into our life.

I tell you these things so you will know there is only one person you need to believe in and follow if you want to be protected, and loved by a power that will never let you down.

I think all of us from time to time have a deep feeling or a voice that tells us not to do something and when we ignore it disaster happens.

I will share one more example for you so that you can identify with it. When in my 30's I was doing real estate. In our office, we had a young couple who went through an example of why listening is so important.

These people were newlyweds in their early 20's. We lived in the Sierra Foothills.

This woman and her husband had gone to a meeting and were leaving about the same time. The woman left first and then her husband would follow in a few minutes.

The woman left a few minutes early from their meeting and headed back to town. The road was curvy but not terribly winding. The woman was driving along a road that she knew. When she went to pick up her cell phone, she dropped it on the floor onto the passenger side. She heard this quiet voice that said don't pick it up, just wait. She said, "I can do this" and she leaned down to passenger floor to pick up her phone and she lost control of the truck and went over an embankment and crashed at the bottom of the hill.

Her husband came by shortly after that but saw no evidence of a crash or someone going off the road. As he drove into the town where they were supposed to meet, He sees a tow truck in front of him as he moves to go around him, he sees his wife's truck all mangled on the tow truck!

He stops the truck driver, and he tells him that the truck he was carrying was his wife's. He shakingly yelled at the man where is my wife! The driver replied "no one was with the truck when I got to it. You must go back to the town where you were and see if she is at the hospital there."

The man jumps in his car and heads back to the town they originally were in and finds out that an ambulance had just returned from an accident on the same road that he was just on looking for his wife. He goes to the only hospital and finds out that his wife is there and in critical condition. He was told she had broken her back and may never walk again.

The blessing in that accident was that she did not die, and I am sure there were many lessons for them to learn due to this accident.

A month or two later, I saw them, and she was frail and still lovely but, in a wheelchair, in her twenties and needed her husband to help her with everything as she could not walk.

I believe that they live because they have something to do for God as he will protect them. A very sad story but another way of showing you that you must listen and follow the quiet inner nudge/voice, as it is God trying to direct you. Listen, Listen.

We are his people, and he wants only the best for us. We must not get caught up in all the chatter and noise that interferes in our life.

CHAPTER

XI

Pay Attention to WHAT YOU'RE SAYING!

Have you ever said a prayer or just simply ask God for his help and what you wanted never happened? If you think about it, you probably added something on to the request after you were done asking, like :

"Watch I won't get what I want, he probably doesn't even hear me".

Whatever we say we create, that is why we must be so very careful. Our comments after what we pray for are very important.

Listening is so important.

You realize that taking time off work could get some negative talk about you not doing your share or whatever would come into your mind that is negative.

Realize that it is the inner voice inside your head that gives you all the negative feelings and thoughts. It is your saboteur that brings negative things your way.

When God is talking, it is a soft voice and/or strong feeling that you can't erase.

CHAPTER XII

Your Own COMPUTER

Have you ever heard the saying that the Brain/Mind is like a computer, it gives you exactly what you put into it. A bit scary when we think about the many things we say and do.

If we are negative, it creates negative. If we confirm something powerful it will happen. We must just know and not be counting the days, as that alone will turn on the doubt that we don't want to have.

I have experienced changing much of what I say or do just by declaring the first thing each morning especially when driving in lots of traffic and people, all pushing to get to work.

I will just declare and give thanks to God. For making this day a very good day. God is who I talk to.

You can do the same thing, saying. "OK Universe", which is God's creation for us to enjoy Life.

Make a Statement:

"Today, everything is going to go well, and this will be a great day, thank you, thank you". I've been told that if you say, "Thank you, Father", he responds and meets your needs." I have seen it over and over even in little things like "Where's my car keys".

You immediately let go of your thought and watch, it will come to be.

I live in a town that has quite a bit of traffic and crazy drivers. I truly hate driving in traffic. I had gone across town on all these traffic roads and for the first time for me, every light that I came upon would turn green right when I got to it.

I knew that it had to be a gift from God so I would be relieved from the stress it gives me.

CHAPTER XIII

Affirming HAPPINESS

Think about trivial things that you can do that make you smile or someone else. Have you ever noticed that when you make someone else smile that it is hard not to smile either on your inside or the smile everyone can see. Just doing things that bring a smile is a healing of kindness on the outside as well as the inside.

Example:

You walk through a park and see a plant with flowers on it. You pick one of the flowers and take it over to an older person or someone just sitting on a park bench. Hand it to them and wish them a good day. In variably they will return the smile.

An example would be on a particular Christmas when my grandchildren, their mom, and myself went to help hand out clothing to the needy for Christmas.

I was amazed at all the people who came for a handout for mostly clothing. Extremely poor people yet they were smiling as we gave them clothes, purses, ties, even a few suits for those looking to go to an interview.

This is one of the things I did not normally do and yet I have never forgotten the happy faces of those that were getting all these gifts. Everyone was pleasant and no rowdiness happened at all.

I think that some of us are so blessed that we never realize that just giving someone a pair of socks when they have none is such a special gift.

It seems that in life as time passes by, we forget that it truly is kindness that is the strongest thing we could give another.

Miracles begin by giving with no expectation of return. Open your heart with love and kindness and happiness follows.

Always remember that giving weather it is your time, your smile or just being generous to not only others, but to yourself creates peace and strength within you when you feel you have none.

Sometimes it can be nothing more than wrapping up in your favorite blanket with one of your favorite books and just letting the negatives float away from you.

When you're sitting in that chair alone and your mind wants to go to the dark places within you, the places that you worry about. Instantly, see yourself open a doorway, it can be a double doorway or a whatever you can create, see it open and let all the darkness flow out the door into the light and quickly dissolve.

Now let a bright white light come down covering the doorway and sealing it from darkness that brings you down. Give thanks for the release of all that does not serve you. You will feel much lighter and happier.

Remember that you do not even have to say what is bringing you down. Just declare that all things that bring you down have disappeared. Only light and good things come through the door to you.

If you have a tablet, notepaper, steno book anything that you can write in and let go of the darkness. If you find you are writing dark thoughts that weigh you down, take your pen or pencil and cross it out. This releases it from your energy and space.

After you cross out the negative then write down what you would like if you had no limitations. Think about what you write. Are you writing things that automatically make you smile or are you writing down things that others have told you that you need.

Understand that if you write down things that others think is best for you, that won't work if you have no interest or desire within you regarding the idea they are offering.

If you follow their suggestion and have no heart for it, you will be forcing yourself to please another and not your own soul, your dreams, and what you would like to be known for.

Confirm that the open space is open for the good uplifting thoughts and ideas that are leading you to your heart's desires. Those may be the thoughts "I wish I could" or even a quiet dream you have within yourself.

Do not be afraid to go ahead and learn or practice what would fulfil your dream. If you want to build cars do so, even if you begin with model cars that come in a box. You will find yourself engaged in what you are doing. If you want to sing keep singing in the shower, at church or anywhere you can lift the spirits of others.

You will find your dream and hope. Never doubt yourself or your dreams.

If you are a writer or artist, use the rest of this page to write or draw something that makes you feel happy and peaceful.

CHAPTER XIV

The Hearts
DESIRE

There are times that we get into a place where we find that we have a lot of capabilities and can do many things. However, we seem to still keep trying all different kinds of things but never finding one that we can't wait to get up in the morning and do.

I think all of us have a desire to be known for something that literally moves us. I think we could compare it to hearing a great singer or musician who just rocks you and takes you to another place with their talent. I think even great art – painting, photography, etc. can do that.

I find that my greatest loves have to do with animals, plants, and nature. Being a mom was something I did that gave me a wonderful feeling of love for my children. However, that was not the whole of me as I have always been that person who was very independent and determined to do great things.

The interesting thing is that the things that made my heart sing were not encouraged by family, friends or whatever. So, I would lose gusto and put those things on a back burner or let others who thought they knew what I should do to be happy lead me to many challenges and incompletions in my life.

Sometimes those of us who have a tender, loving heart find that we can be manipulated by others, only because we want them to be happy with us. So, we tend to try a lot of things that we are never really into or that make us fulfilled.

CHAPTER XV

Finding Your WAY

It is when we are older that we begin to realize that all that we put our heart and soul into and all that we did for those we love was never the answer for our constant smile.

It seems to me that it is when we get older, and the children are adults, and we now have grand children who like/love grandma and grandpa, but they are growing and developing their own lives.

Now as older adults we must figure out what we want and are going to do with our own lives.

You see life just goes on and on, and we must find an identity for ourselves that makes us smile a lot.

I personally have written all my life but never was encouraged to do anything about it. I have many stories that I can present. Writing and storytelling really make me feel happy and loving what I do. It almost seems natural to me.

Will I be a number one selling author? I would like that, but it is not the reason I write. I write because it is what brings me joy and happiness, being able to tell stories that will help others to have a happier and better life.

A Happier and Better Life should be on a list you have to meet your desires. Use this page to write down what really brings a smile to your face.

CHAPTER XVI

The Apple ORCHARD

This is a story that was told to me as a true story, about a man who worked long and hard building a career and great success in his life in the corporate world.

Now this man had worked from a young man to a retired aged man. He never wanted anything as he had more money than he felt he or anyone else probably needed.

After 30 years of working this man retired and moved from the large city back to the country.

He had a beautiful home overlooking the ocean that fulfilled his needs as a business owner, however, that is not where his heart was. He had a longing to return to the country he knew as a young man. He retired from his lifelong business and returned to the country living .

One rare Sunday one of Paul's old friends came to visit. He had heard that his friend had retired.

As they sat and talked on the porch of his country home, they had this conversation. For the sake of Names, we will use John the friend and Paul the retired man.

John mentioned what a tremendous change it was for Paul to leave his lifelong business and move back to the country living.

Paul smiled and said "you know people would think that I was as happy as I could be. You know, looking at the past 30 years, I can honestly say that I've never truly was happy.

I have all this money, this beautiful piece of property and a great home. I have a loving family, and something is "missing". I just never feel happy."

John asked him, "has there ever been a time that you just found yourself smiling?

The man said, "yes there is something that makes me smile. Do you want to see?"

Paul nodded and walked with his friend to the back of his friend's property where there was a small grove of apple trees. His friend walked out into the grove and turned around with a big smile on his face as he pointed to the trees in the grove.

"This is where I cannot make myself not smile. My heart sings and my lips won't quit smiling." He laughed out loud.

John said, "my friend do you not realize that your smile is in the apple orchard, growing and caring for apples and sharing them with others?" Paul picked up an apple and threw it to John.

Paul shook his head and smiled, "I guess you are right. All the time it was under my nose, and I never realized it till just now! He shook his head and said "you know my grandpa told me that I had to find something that would make me a living and give me security. He told me this 50 years ago.

I only saw it as an orchard that grew apples but never thought of it as anything more. I thought it was just about farming for our friends and family.

John said "So my friend now that you are retired why don't you create your own Apple "Business". Paul said "I don't want corporate life any longer.

"John told Paul to just think about it. They parted that night and didn't see each other for about three years."

CHAPTER XVII

Three Years LATER

Out of the blue "John received a Note from Paul asking him to stop by that he wanted to show him something."

When John arrived at Paul's house and looked down the path where they had walked to Paul's orchard, it was now a dirt road with a large barn at the end and a few cars parked near where the barn was.

John drove to the barn and honked his horn. He hardly recognized Paul. He looked younger and was in overalls and wearing a huge smile.

John jumped out of the truck, "so you've gone back to work?

Paul said, "Work?" No, just doing what I love. I don't advertise, just grow apples. The people come from all over and buy large bags to barrels of what I have. I started with a few baskets of apples.

I would sit out front near the driveway and I had a basket there just to see what would happen. People would stop, grab some apples, and drop money in the bucket.

The people coming for apples grew and grew. I finally put up a large barn and made a driveway and put larger amounts of apples back here in the barn and they would come and pay any price for the apples. They said they were great! They all pay cash and I make a good living doing what I love!"

John smiled and kicked the toe of his shoe in the dirt. "Yup, I think you did the right thing. Good move Bud".

He smiled and went to his truck, opened the door, and said "See you in a few. Stay in touch." He waved and drove off.

CHAPTER XVIII

Doing What YOU LOVE

There is truly something to this. Think about it when you were young, if you had a chance to go roller skating, horseback riding, Ice skating, you could get ready quick enough to go.

The interesting thing is when we are doing what we love we can't quit smiling! I would recommend that you take some time and think about or better yet, write down what things make you smile. What are the things that when you think about it make you smile?

If someone said to you let's go fishing, hiking, biking, swimming or to the movies would you be smiling?

Make a list of what makes you smile.

A LIST:

- Writing

- Painting

- Photography

- Horseback Riding/Competing

- Ice Skating

- Cooking

- These are some examples, please make your own list.

What don't you like doing?

B: LIST:

- Science Class
- Cleaning the House
- Painting and Decorating a House
- Building a house
- Pulling Weeds
- Lying on the Beach and Baking
- Having to cook a meal.
- Slopping the pigs
- Milking the cows

Make your own lists and keep them where you can find them and review. It could be that Your tastes may change, however, the things that make you smile will always be there.

If your heart skips a beat and makes you feel super happy, then pursue. Do not let other people's ideas for you become your identity.

If you are good at something dancing, singing, planting gardens, whatever it is? Do not turn your back on it. Your gifts could be the reason that you were born and chosen to share your gifts with others. When we share with others something that we love it feeds you and them. The things you came here to do when you were born are in place to become the things that keep you smiling.

Final Thoughts:

Start a journal, write in it the good things you desire and what you want to let go of.

When you are feeling low, write about it and then follow it up with what you want.

Any negative thoughts you have, write them down and then Draw a line through them and say, "I release this from my life". Then follow it up with what you want and write down:

My hearts desires are:

Write them down and remember to give thanks for your desires and the goodness that is coming into your life.

On all negative and dark thoughts, you have drawn, be sure to draw a line through them and in big letters state":

"I RELEASE!" and then cross out the negative statements.

If something negative in feeling or in reality is coming into you, see it quickly being removed by white light that you bring into you between your body, your mind, and spirit, and then release the thought. Release, Release and see it disappear.

My best wishes to all of you.

www.ingramcontent.com/pod-product-compliance
Lightning Source LLC
LaVergne TN
LVHW020414070526
838199LV00054B/3612